MP3 Players

Jeanne Sturm

Rourke

Publishing LLC

Vero Beach, Florida 32964

www.rourkepublishing.com

PHOTO CREDITS: © Ivan Stevanovic: Title Page; © Rafal Zdeb: page 4; © Jacom Stephens: page 6; © George Peters: page 7; © Norman Bruderhoter (wikipedia.com): page 8; © Jorge Barner (wikipedia.com): page 9; © Isis (wikipedia.com): page 10; © Andres Balcazar: page 13; © Tamás Ambrits: page 14; © scubabartek: page 15; © rjc flyer (wikipedia.com): page 19 top; © Tomaz Levstek: page 20; © 4 x 6: page 23 top; © korhan hasim isik: page 22; © blaneyphoto: page 23 bottom; © Matjaz Boncina: page 25; © Ana Abejon: page 26; © Roman Kobzarev: page 29; © bunnylady: page 30; © Scott Dunlap: page 31; © Sándor Kelemen: page 36; © Doconnell: page 37 bottom; © Krysztof Kwiatkowski: page 37 top; © Craig Lopetz: page 39 middle; © Anatoly Vartonov: page 41; © Michael Krinke: page 42; © Sean Locke: page 43; © Sami Suni: page 44; © Hasan Shaheed: page 45;

Editor: Nancy Harris

Cover Design by Nicola Stratford, bdpublishing.com

Interior Design by Renee Brady

Library of Congress Cataloging-in-Publication Data

Sturm, Jeanne.
  MP3 players / Jeanne Sturm.
     p. cm. -- (Let's explore technology communications)
  Includes index.
  ISBN 978-1-60472-332-8
  1. MP3 players--Juvenile literature. 2. Sound--Recording and reproducing--Juvenile literature. 3. Music--Juvenile literature. I. Title.
  ML74.4.M6S79 2009
  621.389'33--dc22
                                    2008012979

Printed in the USA

CG/CG

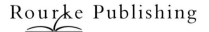

Rourke Publishing

www.rourkepublishing.com – rourke@rourkepublishing.com
Post Office Box 3328. Vero Beach. FL 32964

Contents

MERIDIAN MIDDLE SCHOOL
2195 Brandywyn Lane
Buffalo Grove, IL 60089

CHAPTER ONE

Enjoying Recorded Music

What songs were running through your head earlier today? Are they the same tunes you sang as a young child? Do you think they are similar to the songs your parents enjoy? Your favorite music is probably very different from the music your parents listened to at your age, and your musical tastes have probably changed quite a bit since you were very young. Popular music is always changing as new artists and sounds appear on the scene.

The way we listen to music is also changing. It wasn't so long ago that **CDs (compact disks)** were the newest and best way to enjoy recorded music. Many people carried CD players with them when they walked or jogged, so they could always hear their favorite artists. Before CD players, joggers might have listened to music on a personal **cassette** player or small radio.

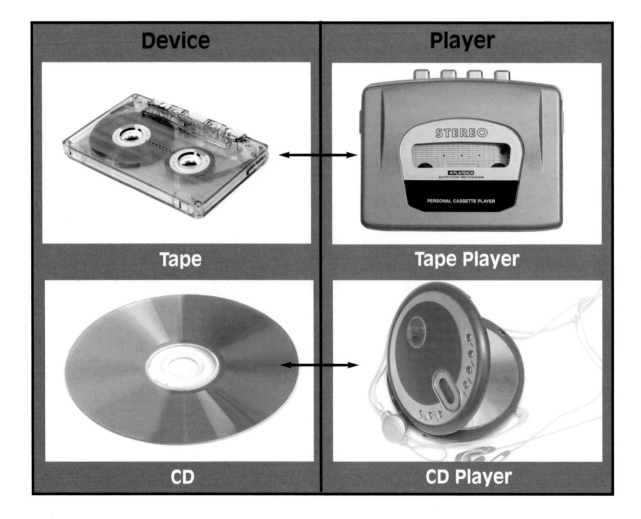

Device	Player
Tape	Tape Player
CD	CD Player

There were limitations to cassette players and CD players, though. If you were going for a walk, you would place one CD in your CD player. During a long walk, you might listen to the same disk two or three times. To be able to enjoy a variety of music, you would have to carry additional CDs. If you decided to jog for a little while, you'd want to be careful. A sudden jolt might cause your song to skip.

The **MP3** player, introduced in the late 1990s, changed all that. Now, you can listen to any one of thousands of your favorite songs on a small portable MP3 player. No matter where you are—at home, in the car, or flying cross-country on an airplane—your collection of songs can go with you.

CHAPTER TWO

The History of Recorded Music

1877 - Thomas Edison invents the **phonograph**. The machine has two needles, one for recording and one for playback. Recordings are made on a tin foil cylinder.

1887 - Emile Berliner invents the **gramophone**. Recordings are made on flat discs or **albums**. The first record albums are made of glass.

1896 - Radio is invented.

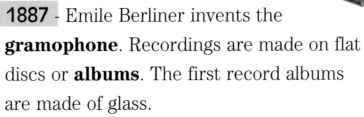

1906 - The first radio broadcast of the human voice is transmitted from Brant Rock, Massachusetts. Sailors at sea across the Atlantic Ocean can hear the words and song.

1934 - Semi Joseph Begun builds first tape recorder for use by the public.

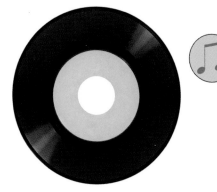

1948 - Columbia Records introduces the first Long Playing (LP) **microgroove** record. It is the standard for decades, and is still in use today.

1949 - RCA (Radio Corporation of America) produces 45-RPM records. These 7-inch recordings play one song on each side.

1954 - The transistor radio is produced. It is the first radio small enough to accompany you wherever you go.

1963 - Cassette tapes are introduced. They are first used for recording **dictation** (words spoken aloud), then become popular for recording music.

1965 - Songs are recorded on 8-track tapes. A plastic outer **cartridge** protects the audiotape.

1969 - The **Internet** is created. Information can be easily transferred from one computer to another.

1979 - The Sony Corporation produces the Walkman, a personal radio and cassette player.

1983 - The Sony and Philips Corporations introduce compact disk (CD) technology.

1986 - Sony develops the MiniDisc. These rewritable disks, smaller than CDs, have anti-skip technology and can be edited easily and quickly.

1989 - The Fraunhofer Institute in Germany patents MP3 format.

1992 - Philips introduces Digital Compact Cassette (DCC).

1998 - The first MP3 players are introduced. Saehan Information Systems sells its MPMan in Korea, and then releases it in the United States as the Eiger Labs MPMan. Diamond Multimedia's Rio is marketed in the United States later the same year.

CHAPTER THREE

How Does MP3 Technology Work?

How is it possible to fit thousands of songs on an MP3 player? It started in the 1970s, when a German research team began working on a way to compress songs to about one-tenth of their size.

The German company, Fraunhofer-Gesellschaft, developed the technology to **digitize** sounds. When sounds are made **digital**, a computer stores each one as a number. Some of the sounds, though, are outside the range of human hearing. MP3 technology removes those sounds. We don't miss them, because we couldn't hear them in the first place.

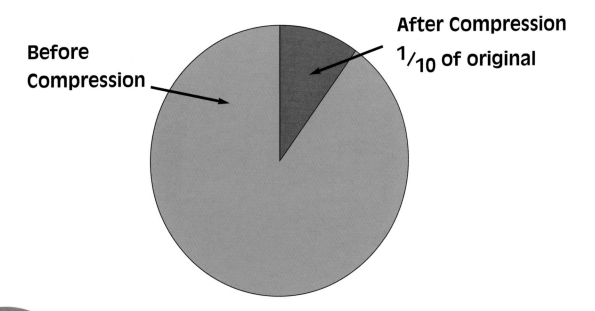

Before Compression

After Compression
$\frac{1}{10}$ of original

What Does MP3 Mean?

MP3 is an abbreviation for MPEG-1 Audio Layer-3. MPEG (pronounced M-peg) is the acronym for Moving Picture Experts Group. It is the name for a group of standards, or guidelines, used for coding compressed audio-visual information. MPEGs role is to keep the technology standard so that it is available to all companies who wish to use it.

Once the music is compressed, it can be transferred through the Internet to your computer.

Technology of your MP3 player

An MP3 player uses software that allows the player to copy
and play songs. MP3 players contain many important
components:

- A data port which allows your MP3 to connect with
  the computer
- Memory, in the form of Flash memory, SmartMedia cards,
  or an internal microdrive
- A **microprocessor**
- A **digital signal processor** (DSP)
- A display
- Playback controls
- A power supply

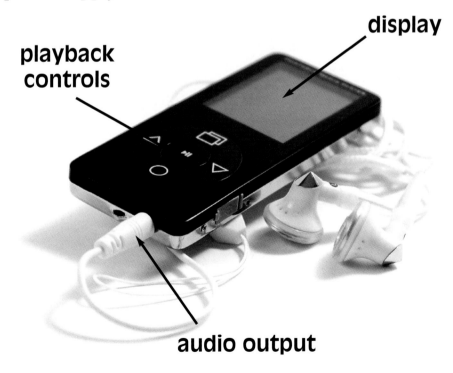

playback
controls

display

audio output

MP3 players can use different forms of memory. It's beneficial to weigh the pros and cons of the different types when purchasing an MP3 player. Internal flash memory, memory sticks, and media cards are all types of solid-state memory, in which there are no moving parts. Memory sticks and media cards can be removed from a player, but internal flash memory is part of the unit. Removable memory sticks and media cards contain varying capacities for memory storage. Cost usually depends on how many **megabytes** or **gigabytes** of memory a consumer wishes to buy. MP3 players that contain hard disk drives can store more memory than players with built-in flash memory, but because hard drives contain some moving parts, they might skip if jostled.

The microprocessor is the brains of the MP3 player. When you use the controls to choose and play a song, the microprocessor sends directions to the digital signal processor (DSP) telling it what to do. The DSP performs the mathematical calculations necessary to decode the digitized music.

CHAPTER FOUR

MP3 Players Through the Years

The first MP3 player, the MPMan, was produced in 1998. It held 32 megabytes (MB) of memory. One megabyte played about one minute of music, so this player couldn't hold many more than eight or nine songs. The unit sold for $250.00, but, for an additional $69.00, you could upgrade your memory to 64 megabytes!

The Diamond Rio, released a couple of months after the MPMan, was also capable of holding 32 megabytes of memory. It ran on a single AA battery. The success of this early MP3 player got the digital music industry rolling.

Kilobytes, Megabytes, Gigabytes

What do we mean when we refer to megabytes and gigabytes of memory? It all starts with a **bit**. A bit is a binary digit. It is used in binary code, a language computers understand, that uses only two digits, 0 and 1, to process information.

A bit is a basic unit of information storage, or memory. A string of eight bits makes a byte. A byte holds only a very small amount of information, so we usually talk about memory in terms of kilobytes (KB), which is 1,024 bytes; megabytes (MB), which is 1,048,576 bytes; and gigabytes (GB), about 1 billion bytes.

In the summer of 1999, the first player with 64 megabytes of built-in memory was released, the Sensory Science RaveMP 2100. It included an expansion slot that would allow a user to add memory, for a total of 96 megabytes. Listeners could enjoy about 90 minutes worth of songs before they'd have to repeat their favorites. This player also included a built-in microphone, so users could record their voices onto the unit.

The first MP3 player to hold more than 20 songs at a time was the Remote Solutions Personal Jukebox (PJB-100), released in the fall of 1999. Designers replaced the flash memory with the hard drive from a laptop. The player, with 4.8 gigabytes (GB) of memory in its **hard drive**, could now hold 1200 song files. It was large and heavy and, at $799.00, quite costly. But the technology was groundbreaking. It is still used in most of today's much smaller MP3 players.

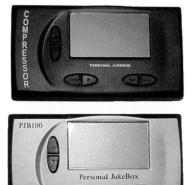

The iPod, produced by Apple, first appeared on the scene in October 2001 with a 5-gigabyte (GB) hard drive. Different from any other MP3 device, the iPod featured a scroll wheel on the front of the player. Rather than repeatedly pushing buttons to find a song, listeners could simply spin the wheel to scroll through their music libraries.

The first iPod cost $399.00. It worked only with Apple's Macintosh computers. But a second model, released in July 2002, was compatible with Windows, as well. It could now be used on PCs (Personal Computers). It also boasted more memory, with a 20 GB hard drive.

Apple Product Release

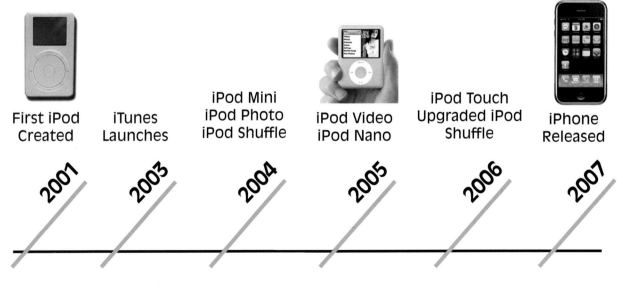

First iPod Created	iTunes Launches	iPod Mini iPod Photo iPod Shuffle	iPod Video iPod Nano	iPod Touch Upgraded iPod Shuffle	iPhone Released
2001	2003	2004	2005	2006	2007

In October 2004 Apple released the color iPod Photo. This player had a color display and larger battery. While enjoying downloaded music, listeners could browse through a collection of their favorite photos. The iPod Photo also displayed a picture of the album cover of the song currently being played.

Two new iPods were released in 2005, the tiny nano in September, and a video iPod in October. Besides a library of songs, both of these new players held a calendar and address book, along with games and a screen saver.

The much-anticipated iPhone was released in June 2007. Unlike previous iPods, it had no scroll wheel. There were no buttons to dial the phone. Instead, the iPhone employed a touchscreen. With an iPhone, you could use wireless technology **(Wi-Fi)** to surf the Internet, check e-mail, and shop at the iTunes store. Once you located a Wi-Fi hot spot, you could preview, buy, and **download** songs, TV shows, and videos.

CHAPTER FIVE

Choosing an MP3 Player

Deciding to buy an MP3 player is easy. Figuring out which one you want can be a little more difficult. There are different types of MP3 players. They are grouped by how they store their media.

Flash memory players are smaller and lighter than hard drive players.

Will you be using the player when you run? You'll want one with a flash memory instead of a hard drive. You can use the flash memory inside the unit, or you can use removable memory cards. Because there are no moving parts, players with flash memory can handle some bumps and jolts. They also use less battery power, so you'll be recharging less often.

Hard drive players are larger and heavier than flash memory players, but they can store many more songs. You could store your entire music collection on a hard drive player and still have room for photos and video.

Hard drive players do have some moving parts, so they may skip when jolted. However, many players are equipped with anti-skip protection to solve that problem.

MP3 CD players are CD players that play MP3 and other digital files. These are cheaper than flash memory and hard drive memory players, but they are also much larger. They might skip when bumped, so they wouldn't be a good choice for sportsmen or runners.

Besides storing digital music, a MiniDisc MP3 player can store data files from your personal computer.

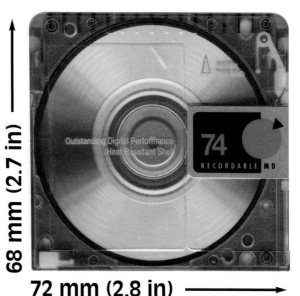

68 mm (2.7 in)

72 mm (2.8 in)

Do you have a project due at school? Make it a power point presentation. No more worries about getting a large display board to school in one piece. You can take your presentation to school on your MiniDisc player!

Before you purchase an MP3 player, try it out. Make sure you understand how to use the on-screen display. Will you be able to find your favorite songs?

How is the sound quality? It's not a bad idea to bring a set of headphones to the store to test the sound quality of different players. You're going to be listening to a lot of music on your player, so make sure you're happy with what you hear.

Many players are equipped with an FM **tuner**. This is a nice option. After all, sometimes you'll want to listen to the radio to hear the newest releases from your favorite artists.

CHAPTER SIX

Enjoying MP3 Technology

Most of us think of music when we think of MP3 players. We can visit an **online music store** to purchase new songs and albums. Even better, we get to hear some of each song before we buy, so there's less chance of spending money on music we don't really like.

Online music stores sell individual songs and complete albums. You can search for a specific band or singer, or you can shop by **genre**. Apple's online store, iTunes, offers music choices such as rock, pop, and country. You can also browse through lists of movies, TV shows, music videos, podcasts, iPod games, and more.

Many more online stores, such as BuyMusic, MusicMatch, Sony, and Wal-Mart, sell songs, albums, music videos, TV shows, and short films. Some of these sites allow you to pay a monthly subscription fee of about $15.00 for all the music you want.

Once you've set up an account with an online music store, the real fun begins. One of the best features of owning an MP3 player is setting up a playlist. You can sort all your favorite songs by genre, by artist, or even by the mood certain songs fit. A playlist can be as short as one or two songs, or as long as your entire list of music.

Playlists let you play the part of the disc jockey, rearranging your songs, sorting them, and skipping through them whenever you wish.

Want to fill up your MP3 files quickly, but can't afford to pay for music from an online store? What about all those CDs you've collected over the years? You can use ripper and encoder software to copy the songs from your CD to your computer's hard disk. The ripper copies the sound to your computer's hard drive. The encoder compresses the song into MP3 format, and you can download it to your MP3.

Another way to enjoy your MP3 player is with audiobooks. You're probably familiar with books on cassette tape or CD. Many people listen to them in their cars on long-distance trips or daily commutes. With MP3 technology, you can purchase audiobooks through an online store, just as you purchase music. Thousands of titles are available online.

Once you've bought a book and downloaded it to your MP3 player, you can listen whenever and wherever you like.

Podcasts are another popular way to use an MP3 player. Podcasts are programs that you can download and enjoy any time you choose. They include newscasts, magazine reports, and television shows.

CHAPTER SEVEN

Beyond the Basics

MP3 players are not just about digital data any more. Many MP3 players come equipped with added features, including FM radio tuners, built-in microphones for recording, and adapters that allow your MP3 music to play on your car stereo.

Additionally, other types of electronic devices are building MP3 capabilities into their units. Besides the iPhone, many other cell phones now have built-in MP3 players. Your cell phone provider might allow you to download music over its network. How many songs you can download depends on your phone, but many allow use of an external memory card, giving you more options.

What if you want all the features of the iPhone, without the phone? Check out the iPod Touch, where you still enjoy all the benefits of built-in Wi-Fi (wireless technology). With your iPod Touch, you can surf the Internet and access iTunes for all of your favorite songs, videos, TV shows, and podcasts.

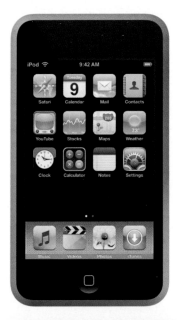

The Sansa Shaker is a fun unit for kids. It is equipped with a speaker so you can share your music with a group of people, but it also has two headphone jacks so you and a friend can listen without disturbing anyone else in the room. The Shaker plays songs like any other MP3 player, but when you want to change songs, you can just shake the device. It automatically switches to a new selection.

Other MP3 players offer lots of features at a nice price. The Sansa Clip player comes with a built-in microphone. It also plays FM radio stations and audiobooks, and includes a screen so you can see your files as you browse. The Sansa View adds movies, TV shows, and videos, along with the ability to enjoy your own collection of photographs.

Microsoft's Zune includes Wi-Fi, an FM tuner, and a screen where you can watch videos and browse through your photos. The Wi-Fi allows you to share favorite songs with other Zune owners.

How would you like a Swiss Army Knife that plays music? It really exists! It's called the s.beat, and it comes with 1, 2, or 4 gigabytes of memory and a rechargeable battery that lasts for eight hours. The s.beat comes with voice recording capabilities and has a built-in FM radio. You can even record FM radio onto your player. Want to share a favorite song with a friend? You can, with the s.beat's two earphone jacks.

Outdoor adventurers rely on GPS (Global Positioning System) units to help them find their way in unfamiliar areas. A basic GPS receiver can tell them where they are and how to get to their destination. But some units make it even more fun by including extra features. The Magellan Triton 2000, for example, includes a camera, a compass, a flashlight, a voice recorder, and an MP3 player. It's even waterproof, in case hikers get caught in a sudden downpour.

Runners might enjoy Timex's watch, the Ironman iControl. They can plug a small receiver into their iPod, and the iControl on their wrist becomes a remote control. Wearers can skip or repeat songs, adjust the volume, and pause the music when necessary. The Ironman is still a sport watch, though, so it continues to include features runners rely on, such as computing average and best times for the run.

You can wear the Sony S2 Sports Walkman strapped to your arm. Separate your playlist into fast songs for running and slower songs for walking. The player will automatically switch from one playlist to the other when you stop walking and start to run. The sports function tracks how many steps you've taken and how many calories you burned during your run.

CHAPTER EIGHT

Cool Gear for Your MP3 Player

Your MP3 player is made for portability. It is small and lightweight. Sometimes, though, you want to share music with friends, or listen without wearing the earbuds that came with your player. Many fun and useful accessories are sold to help you enjoy your music to the fullest.

Speakers and Headphones

Some headphones are made to cover your ears.

You can purchase additional earbuds to match the color of your player.

Speakers plug in to the earphone jack on an MP3 player and allow the music to play throughout the room.

Docking Stations

Docking stations keep MP3 players charged and ready to go. They also provide audio output with stereo quality sound. One model connects wirelessly to your home stereo. Docking stations allow you to enjoy your MP3s in your home, hands free!

Child Friendly Mp3 Players

They appear to be toys, but the raised dots on these building block look-alikes are actually control buttons for an MP3 player!

The built-in speaker on the Sansa Shaker allows you to share music with family and friends. Give it a quick shake and you've got a new song.

The Max-Joy is very child friendly, with it's large buttons for little fingers to operate. It also limits audio output so it won't hurt little ears.

Waterproof MP3 Headphones

What would you listen to underwater? Whale songs, maybe!

MP3 in your Car Stereo

Connect to your car's audio system and you can listen to all your favorites, commercial free!

With MP3 technology, we can find favorite songs no longer sold in stores, carry thousands of songs with us wherever we go, and organize our music by artist or genre.

We can listen to entire books read aloud, view movies and television shows, and download podcasts of favorite radio programs.

Grab your tennis racket or load up your car for a holiday. Wherever you go, your MP3 player is ready to go along!